Poetry in Motion

A few bribes later and this is what people have been saying ...

'Dai Woolridge is a creative genius with a heart-full of Jesus. A lyrical acrobat and a gospel ninja. I'm proud to be a friend and a fan!'

DAI HANKEY
(Author of 'Offensive', Pastor of Hill City Church)

'Dai's poetry communicates God's truth in a way that is funny, fresh and faithful. If you're directed to 'Left/Right' or find yourself chuckling through 'The builder's bum', he always points you back to the great grace of God.

'This is a book that you'll come back to time and time again - to laugh, to be comforted, or just plain inspired. Either way, a great resource if you want something "special" for a church service.'

JOHNATHAN THOMAS
(Pastor of Ammanford Evangelical Church)

'A creative God-centered series of original and fresh, contemporary poetry kept sharp and to the point by the author's up-to-date 21st century metaphors, ranging from downloadable apps to a builder's bum. Many of Dai's personal psalms are perfect for congregational use and help keep the Christian Creative Arts truly creative and yet accessible to all. His rhythmic use of language is incarnational throughout and lands without need of further translation into our modern culture. If you like good poetry you will love this volume. If you don't like good poetry this volume might change your mind.'

KEVIN ADAMS
(Author of 'A Diary of Revival', East Baptist Church Lynn MA. USA)

'Words have power. Power to heal, power to wound, power to make us stop in our tracks or change direction. A poet's words can slip under our defences and show us a reality that we had not perceived before. Delivered with anointing they can cut to the heart with truth, love, forgiveness and mercy. They can change our faith-horizon forever.

'I have had the privilege of hearing Dai Woolridge perform many of these scripts and have seen the results in people's faces and people's hearts. It is a joy to commend them to you. Don't just read them; perform them, and watch what our amazing God does!'

ROY GODWIN
(The Fflad-Y-Brenin TRUST, Author of 'Grace Outpouring')

'Just occasionally you come across somebody that you realise has been exceptionally gifted by God. It's not just that these people are wonderful preachers, singers or youth workers: they have something else. I have no doubt that Dai Wooldridge has that mysterious something. Yes he is a brilliant poet, yes he is a wonderful communicator, but … so much more.'

ROB PARSONS
(Founder and Chairman of 'Care for the family', best selling author of 'Bringing home the prodigals')

'Dai Woolridge is an actor and writer who marries passion with performance and playfulness with prayer. He is shaped by three qualities that are as essential to writing as they are to faith - he loves God, he loves people and he loves words. This sparkling collection is a valuable resource and a welcome addition to the postmodern library of prayer.'

GERARD KELLY
(International speaker, Author of 'Twittergies' and 'Spoken Worship')

Poetry in Motion is moving. In every sense. Dai's words bounce and skip and teeter and twist and bang into your head and into your heart.

BOB HARTMAN
(Professional storyteller, Author of 'The Wolf That Cried Boy!')

'Dai has an infectious passion for life in all its fullness and a beautiful desire to pass it on. His unique way of looking at the world is shared with great gusto in this winsome collection.'

ABBY GUINNESS
(Author of 'The Word of the Wives', Head of Creative Arts for Spring Harvest)

Poetry in Motion

*50 Daily Readings of 21st Century Psalms -
for Worship, Prayer and Performance*

Dai Woolridge

*Follow Dai on Twitter :
@twitwitandgrit*

This title is also available as an e-book product
(ISBN: 978-0-9571276-1-6)

Front cover and Interior design by Marc Thomas
http://thatisjustawesome.com

Printed by imprintDigital.net

ISBN: 978-0-9571276-0-9

Published by twitwitandgrit
PO Box 2441,
Cardiff
CF23 0BN

For my beautiful Cath

(Not just because she wants to be my first dedication, but because she is my helper.)

Inspired by the late, great wordsmith himself, Rob Lacey.

Contents

He chooses me
He is my
The only shout out worth shouting about

Postmodern Psalms of Prayer
Fix me
Elevate
My prayer
Lord give me
Lord I feel like a double
Your day/Your way
Counting down the hours

Questions/Answers
What did you expect?
What's it all about?
Judge or be Judged?
Which Luke do you want to be?

Desert Place
Be raw, be real, be you
I'm flat
Let him in
Out of place
It figures

Topics
Rich (Wealth)
Justice (Justice)
It's not (Grace)
Map it out (Choice)
3 in 1 (Holy Trinity)

Festive poetry
The real Christmas story poem
The ickle King of the Crib
X marks the spot

Foreword by Paul Francis

I have known Dai for nearly ten years. The first time I met him I realised that this boy, well man, had creativity dripping from every pore. He could write and act in a way that moved you from laughter to tears and back again. Sure in those days he was very 'raw' but it was obvious that God was shaping Dai. And so I have watched how Dai has developed and grown over this time, creating new shows, writing performance poetry and mentoring younger aspiring 'creatives'.

And now to this book, which is a culmination of many years' writings. It is all Dai would like it to be:

Inspiring
Challenging
Uplifting
Refreshing
Honest

But above all, these poems, contemporary psalms and thoughts encourage us into a greater encounter with and a love for God. Dai has a real love for the Bible and one of his desires is that he takes some of the big themes and presents them in a new way that is accessible to both seekers and scholars. So he uses everyday items such as cars, pens, apps and mobile phones to tackle some of these great themes - God's love, the cross, brokenness and the poor, just to mention a few.
The versatility of this book means that you can use it in many ways. You could use this for personal meditations, or as part of a small group meeting, or in large gatherings. Whichever way, the poems will evoke a response from readers/listeners as they connect with what most people experience through life. I encourage you to use this book from the 'Praise Psalms' to the 'Desert Place' because that is life as we all know it!
May you find here a pool of refreshment as you encounter the living God through the words.

Paul Francis
(Director of 'Going Public' and Pastor of Glenwood Church, Cardiff)

Acknowledgements

Thanks to ...

Carol and Alexa for all your encouragement and help with editing the book.

Gerard, Rob, Dai, Jon, Abby, Roy, Bob and Kev for your kind words.

Als and Jan – Als, for your love, support and creative input that makes me better, and for challenging me not to settle for average. Jan, for all your encouragement over the years, for all that you've invested in me right from my teens, for the games that wouldn't pass health and safety checks today!

Paul 'just pick the car up from Nice airport' Francis for being a great example of a leader and a friend. For all your input, for seeing my potential, believing in me and giving me many opportunities.

Roberto Burns for all your encouragement and for being a great mentor and a friend.

Kev the rev for your teaching and for first giving me a passion for drama. The way you actively 'do' relationship with God in a way that is faithful to scripture, yet outside the mould, is a big inspiration. Your creative energy and enthusiasm for drama was and always will be infectious.

JT for your teaching and for all the support you've shown me.

Mark with a 'C' for your genius skill with a MacBook in designing my cover and making the book look good.

To Ads for how much of a friend and a brother you are to me, I will always have a slight man crush on you.

Pete 'caramel macchiato' Joyce - for being my Starbucks buddy, a hazelnut hot chocolate is never the same without you!

Emz and Lis – for being such a big part of our lives. From History lessons through to 'Micah cwtshes' and everything in-between.

To ALL my really good friends, for encouraging and challenging me to be a better man and for doing life with me.

To Sammy Davies and all at AEC for your love, friendship and support

To all at Going Public for 'Going Public' with your love and support, (see what I did there?).

To all at Glenwood Church and the faith community, The National Prayer Breakfast of Wales and Ignite for your support.

A big thanks also to ...

Mam – for all your love and for being a great example of a mother and a faithful servant.

Dad – for your humour and attitude to life despite the tough times; keep on keeping on.

Dylan and Jessica, I'm so proud to be your brother, I love you both to bits.

Walt and PC Gar, you guys are the best in-laws I could've hoped for. Thanks for everything you have done for us.

Thank you to Billy Engel, my creative mentor when I was a student, for making me realise my potential.

Thank you to the late Rob Lacey - you are my creative inspiration.

Special thanks to ...

Cath - for putting up with me, for being my biggest fan. For everything that you are. For your total love, friendship, support, wisdom and cwtches. For your infectious passion for life and for Jesus.

The greatest thanks to ...

My Saviour, for saving a wretch like me.

'Poetry in Motion': 'The Intro'

When I think of 'poetry in motion', a variety of images flick through my mind. I think of Shane Williams any time he's got the ball in an open space, or 'that' famous Barbarians' try versus New Zealand in 1973, when Welsh legend, Gareth Edwards, dives in the corner, as if 'failing to score' never entered his vocabulary.

But there's more activity resembling 'poetry in motion' than mere rugby, even if it is the world's best sport; God appointed! I'm sure if you thought hard enough, you'd come up with a couple of examples yourselves. Maybe for you it's watching Swan Lake … maybe it's just watching swans in a lake.

The point is, when we value something as 'poetry in motion', it's because it moves us and inspires us. It's something that we aspire to, although knowing full well that we'll rarely, if ever, reach it.

So then, I move on from great rugby to the heart of what inspires me most.

I think of David's psalms; his heartfelt conversations with God through string arrangements and poetic prayers. That then moves me to think about what inspired him.

When I truly consider what inspires me and what I dream of aspiring to, I think there's nothing higher and nothing more poetic than the life of my Saviour, Jesus Christ. His life on earth in its essence was 'poetry in motion'; perfect in every way. More than that, He was willing to give up His true status as God divine to restore a broken relationship. He took our death sentence and made the whole of humanity justified in the space of one weekend.

So, being directly inspired by the life of the Saviour, which was 'poetry in motion', I present to you a resource of 'poetry' that seeks to communicate that very thing.

But it doesn't stop there. I invite you to set it into 'motion' yourselves, in the public places and in the quiet places:

Public places - To read it aloud in church services, during worship sets, in small groups, around tables, or anywhere you think could be appropriate and of benefit to others. This collection of poems is meant to journey from ink in a book to words on people's lips.

Quiet places - To digest it in the quiet places of your own time with God. You will find that the poems are split into 50 daily readings for those who are into daily doses - but this is a guideline not a contract. For those who feel more daring, select day 50 and work backwards - or just pick a number and start reading.

So, here are 50 contemporary psalms and poetic prayers, plus the mission statement as to why I've written them. Some are moulded through metaphors and word play; some are specific to topics, whilst others are purely focused on praising our Almighty Father. Ultimately they are to celebrate God and ask big questions, knowing 'He' is the answer.

However you choose to read this collection, I pray that it becomes an accessory that speaks to the heart and points us back to our one true living Maker and Shaper. I pray that these poems will be snacks for the soul.

So whether in coffee shops or worship sets, outreach events or quiet times, I present to you my collection of 21st century psalms and invite you to set 'poetry' into 'motion' …

My Mission Statement ...

To reach, teach and preach,
To be all over the God stuff.

To let the 66 books be the concrete of whatever goes on top of it.

To create, re-create, adapt and update;
To perform for the Big Guy in the clouds
not just for performance sake.

To be all about relevance – relating, creating and imitating
God's love in creative ways

For his glory
For his glory
For his glory.

To connect with those who need connecting;

To inspire the apathetic;
To challenge the 'I've got this God stuff nailed' group.

To big up the humble;
To big even bigger up the Big Man upstairs.

To 21st century the words;
Not mess with the content
But revamp the style,
Lose the tradition to create a new one.
One that speaks the language of the new generation.

To tell the story
Tell the story
Tell the story

Of some guy who died when he was cross
To help me save my hymns?

Nope.

To not get the story wrong.
Flip out the message so people get it, bang on!

To be a soldier for the cause
His cause
His cause;
To sign up to none other than the Holy Guy's clause.

To use my hands in only one way
To big up the Big Man,
To put my hands together
And give God the biggest round of applause.

Metaphors
(Meaty-theological-phors)

Jesus loved his metaphors. He loved telling stories, not just for story sake but to convey a message, the message quite often being 'the kingdom of God' … If not that, then giving us a snippet of the Father's love for us, how he tallies up our debt or how he feels when we come back to him. He did all this through stories; stories, metaphors and then some more stories. Isn't that great? God incarnate was a storyteller! An imagination-grabbing, picture-painting, word-pronouncing storyteller. And that's what I try and do here.

How do I get across 'a love that outranks all sin'? How do I communicate a God whose depth of wisdom I cannot begin to grasp? Well, I don't – but what I do is try and communicate it anyway. Try and make a culturally relevant message culturally relevant, by telling stories and using metaphors. They'll never do him justice, but if they'll just come close – it will be worth it.

Day 1
God in four wheels

He created us, aids us and repairs us.

You're the ultimate car lot owner, taking in any car with any mileage (even Skodas … the old ones).

You valet me
And validate me – inside and out.
You tweak, tune and tone me so I can reach my full potential,
And I only ever reach it when you're behind the wheel.

Bodywork's not your speciality; you're more into the soul and the spirit.
You're not fazed with how fast I do 0-60,
You prefer me being character driven when I do it.

Thank you for saving me from becoming scrap metal,
Thanks for not clamping me when I go on double yellows.

If I choose you to be my insurer –
You're the greatest cos you always insure that I'm yours no matter what.

The ultimate car lot owner,
The greatest car insurer.
And your son – who took the biggest crash
So he can be my roadside recovery.

Day 2

The pretentious pen

We're a glass half empty when it comes to what we have to offer God. But it never was about us. It's about what he can do through us.

The pretentious pen looks after number bic.
It doesn't write on behalf of someone else,
It's far too concerned with running low on ink.

Out of all the thousands of pencils who scribble
their way through life
only to be
rubbed
out,

Bic isn't grateful he writes with ink,
He's in a huff cos he's not a fountain pen.

Bic dreams of an upgrade,
Having the latest in ballpoint technology.

He wants a fancy spring-loaded top
To be clicked on and off at the writer's convenience -
'If I flip my lid one more time ...!'

Bic isn't an over-enthusiastic all-in-one pen
With 5 colour capabilities,
He doesn't come in a snazzy box or have a lifetime guarantee,
And to put it as bluntly as an unsharpened pencil
he's socially inept with ink cartridges.

But when all is read and done
I'm afraid old bic is missing the ball point ...
The writer, the author – the wordsmith himself,
He doesn't see him as a doodler
Or a shopping list pen,
He sees him as an opportunity to write a masterpiece

(... and one that no amount of Tippex can erase).

Day 3
The builder's bum

My faith through a construction site.

I don't want a spiritual builder's bum,
I wanna buckle up the belt of truth so I'm not caught with my trousers down!

I want my Holy Spirit level to be off the charts;
I wanna be the 2 lines and I want the Big Man to be the bubble -
smack bang in the centre.

I can only do this when I'm straight,
with him and myself
Knowing that I'd never measure up by my own handy work,
Only by the carpentry of Christ.

I wanna wear my hard hat at all times
Cos it's the hard hat he gives me that saves me.

I want him to be the foreman:
He says the word and I get on with the job.

I want my relationship with him to be concrete,
No builder's bum (you know, cracks).

I wanna be the wise guy who builds his house upon a rock
Cos he's my cornerstone and my solid foundation.

I want God-given steel toe capped boots
So I can stand firm, ready with the peace of mind that I can face anything.

I want anything that isn't of you, God, to be
Chucked in the skip (recycled in the relevant sections of course).

The grace and love that Christ puts in my wheelbarrow
I wanna be picking out and dropping off
So other builders can be built up in him too –
After all, this stuff will never run out of stock.

Metaphors : Poetry In Motion

God's Word isn't too runny or clumpy,
It's the perfect mix.
Cement perfection.

How much love has he got for us?
There's no measuring tape long enough to find out.
So, before I clock off,
Whatever mess I get myself into -
If I fall off the scaffolding
or get stuck in the rubble -
I know I'm sorted
Cos JC will save me.
JC will dig me out.

Day 4

God – the bank manager

Our sin is wiped clean in Jesus Christ … so we'll never be judged on our credit rating, but on his.

God's like a bank manager – though when he lends you his grace, he doesn't expect it back with interest. Believe it or not – he just wants to get you out of the red and into the black.

He wants to get all the paperwork, all the 'urgent' 'pay now' correspondence and put it in the shredder. No, better than that – he wants to make the ultimate transfer – all the debt from your accounts, one balance transfer – one wired transaction into his. He'll take all your debt off you and pay for it out of his own personal wallet. All you've got to do is call the meeting.

He doesn't want to 'consolidate your loans' – he wants to delete them so they don't even show up on Equifax. He doesn't use fancy words like 'APR' or 'handling fees'.

He doesn't back you into a corner to sign on the dotted line; even if he knows he's the only bank that can sort your sin-terest; he leaves it up to you – it's your call.

He doesn't notify you with a letter that says you went over the agreed forgiveness level.

Why? Because there is no overdraft for his forgiveness limit.

God's like a bank manager – though you can trust him, whatever the climate. If your love for him goes into recession, no difference – he's still there. If you open up an account with him, he's always there, and he'll never terminate your soul bank account.

Day 5

The scruffy caddy

The good news of golf.

He doesn't look much – the scruffy caddy.
If you took one glance at him you'd think he belongs in soup kitchen queues
or down the high street selling Big Issues.

It's not like he wears the regulatory uniform required by members of the golf course,
And his caddy techniques aren't exactly mainstream.
He doesn't use golf head covers,
He uses tube socks from Peacocks.

To look at him, you'd think he wouldn't know the difference between an albatross
and a hole in one on a par 4.

But you should see his game.
Every stroke perfect to a T.
No drop shots necessary,
The only time he spends in the bunker is making sand castles in between shots.

Over the fairway, a bounce or two on the green
And …

Hole in one
Hole in one
Hole.in.one.
He does the record 18-hole course in 18 fluid strokes.

He plays the perfect game
But he makes it out as if we were the ones holding the club.
So it's not his name in the Echo shaking hands with the course chairman;
It's ours.

We vandalised the golf course,
made divots on the greens
and trashed the sprinklers.

The scruffy caddy
Lets us take the credit for the perfect game
But also pays the fine for the damage we caused to the course.

He gets kicked out of the golf club, with a bad rep, ban and restraining order on any course within a 60-mile radius.

And as for us?
We get membership jackets and golf buggies with personalised number plates.
We become committee members of the golf course
And best pals with the course chairman.

Day 6

i-God/There's an app for that

Consumerism tells us it's got the goods, when in actual fact – God's the only thing worth having.

You need restoration? There's an app for that.
You need guidance? There's an app for that.
Need filling, cos the apps you fit aren't fitting?

Guess what?
There's an app for that.

Feel enslaved by your own self-loathing?
Feel less than?
Or more than less than?

Feel trapped by insecurity?
Feel like the only thing you're sure of is doubts?
There's an app
There's an app
There's an app … for that.

This app restores, guides, and makes you fit.
It tells you you're unique.
It gets you
Protects you
And always wants to connect with you.

Need acceptance?
Need purpose?
Clean slate?

There's an app
There's an app
There's an app … for that.

Need love?
Need rest?
Need joy?

There's an app
There's an app
There's an app ... for that.

Need life?
There's an app.

Need it to the full?
There's an app.

This app applies eternity to life;
This app works only via 3G
And it's ready for you to download -

Cos there's an app
There's an app
There's an app ... for that.

The future's bright, the future's origin -
The new origin -
The origin of grace ...

Apply that.

Day 7
The journey

Faith is the longest distance race, but it's worth it for the finishing line.

This journey, it's not just about the milestones,
It's about the every single inch stones,
The rocks, the pebbles and all of the stepping-stones.
It's not just the glory years
or the really rough times -

It's the present, the here, the now
the minute by minute
hour by hour
24/7/52 ever continuing journey with the Almighty.
It's about the lot
The whole caboodle
The biggest journey
The longest distance race.
Not just the finish line
But the every stride it takes to get there.

So, in every stride,
With every heart beat,
In every laugh, in every tear,
In every silence, in every prayer rant;

Here I am
As I am
Running the race
Hoping, just hoping I'll reach the finish line.

Day 8
A world without

A world without God is a world without.

A world without love is like a conductor without rhythm.

A world without hope is like the millennium dome ... (pointless!)

A world without faith is like a Dad's Army catchphrase ... (we're all doomed!)

A world without friendship is like a hiker with masses of flat land.

A world without laughter is like a workaholic without a job.

A world without dreams is like a painter without a canvas.

A world without sense is like a student without an overdraft.

A world without God is a world without ...

Where love is crooked

Where hope is hopeless

Where faith is plain crazy

Where friendship is shallow small talk

Where laughter's just not funny

Where dreams are a nightmare

Where sense is completely and utterly nonsense.

A world without God
Is a world without.

Metaphors : Poetry In Motion

Day 9

Mobile phone

> We're a little bit like mobile phones - once my battery was dead,
> but now it's been charged.

I was dead without you.
Completely and utterly flat
… no life,
not a peep.

I was dead cos I kept calling premium numbers at premium rates that I couldn't afford.

Then he came along, he charged me back to life …
My bars went straight to full.

We both got charged.
He got charged for my astronomical phone bill …
He was on the phone for hours convincing the operator …
Then his battery went dead.

Till 3 days later – he resurrected and fully charged!
He became the universal charger and the only docking system.

I was flat, I was dead … no life, not a peep.
Then he came along and recharged me,
Though I'm not full bars unless he's nearby.
And I still get low
So I go to him – my charger, my docking system.
And when I do I'm full cos the most incredible thing happens:
he keeps paying my bills
and he keeps charging me up.

Wordplay

Words are fun and so diverse. The way they sound when you roll them off the tongue, the syllables, the intonation, the emphasis on pronouncing them, and the way that sometimes the most everyday word looks or sounds alien to us once repeated several times; like 'of' ... of ... OF ... (Hmm, I'm sure you could think of better!)

God has gifted us not only with a personal, living relationship with him, but he's also gifted us with the ability to express it. We were designed with the purpose to praise him, sometimes with words.

This section is focused on trying to give God the worship he deserves through the style of wordplay. These poems are designed to be spoken out as performance pieces. So I hope you enjoy, whether reading to yourself or performing to others.

Day 10

Get God

Receive him and understand him ... the first is one choice,
the latter - a lifetime journey.

Get God
Don't reject God
But get the good news God gives.

Get God
Comprehend him
Try and rack your brains round him
And when you fail to fully get the scope of his beauty,
Get the fact that he cannot fully be 'got'.

Get God
Don't forget God
Get hold of him
Cos he's waiting to get hold of you.

God gets you
He doesn't reject
He doesn't forget.
He just waits
In the hope that one day ... you'll get it.
You're meant to be gotten by the getter – got it?

Good, then go and get him,
Get God.

Wordplay : Poetry In Motion

Day 11

Left/Right

We're only right when he's the centre.

I don't know my right from my left.
Or my left from my right.

I know he's right – God, that is, but I'm just left confused which way that is.

When God is left – I'm not right but on the other hand God is right in my life when I'm left.

He's right – I'm left.
I'm wrong – he's right and I'm only right when I go his way –
the right way and leave behind what should be left, right?

Paul, the New Testament guy, rights about it – left, right and centre – left-eousness through faith … no, that's not right?!

But I do, wanna be right – so he's got to be centre and when he is, I'm left – left with right joy because I know he makes me right – and he radically improves my sight – he gives me scriptural prescription glasses.

So I say when I can see his sovereignty …
'What's better than when he's right? Right at the centre.'

Day 12

The Alpha...bet

God in 26 letters.

A nchor my attitude

B etter my benchmark

C arry my conscious choices

D ent my detrimental ego

E nlighten my eternity

F ish out my falseness

G et my God spot

H one my humility

I nch forward my innings

J ar up my jealousy

K ill off my kicking off

L aminate my life as I live it for your love

M ake my manhood meet your measures

N egate my negativity

O perate on my open wounds

P rotect my patience not my portions

Q uicken my quest for answers to my questions

R ecover my readiness to read your Word daily

Sustain my satisfaction in you alone

Turn my trust to you

Unveil my undivided attention

Veer my choices away from vengeance

Wake up my wisdom

Xtinguish my self afflicting xtermination

Yell your way Yahweh

Zeal me up; for the Alpha...bet.

Day 13
One

There's only one.

One King
Although one servant

One law
Although one fulfilment

One chance to change the course of history
One lifetime though one eternity

One life
One destiny

One cross
One death

One resurrection
One true love and affection

One life lived to perfection

One ultimate sin correction
One uncontainable love protection

One ascension
The one and only
King … did I mention?

Day 14

The Way

The way, the truth, the light – end of.

There's more than one way to skin a cat
But there's only one way to God's grace.

There are many ways to eat a Cadbury's cream egg
But there's only one true way to get full forgiveness that desecrates the hold of sin.

There are many ways to save the pennies
But only one way to save your soul.

There are vast volumes of literature to learn from
But only one way to get into God's good books.

There are many religions that say they've got the Heaven pass
But only one is valid at the pearly gates.

The one that knows that if we'd be merited by the rulebook
We wouldn't have a hope.

Many ways to do religion
But one way to do it right
By not even doing it – but by doing faith.

Faith in one guy,
That he took the rap for us,
That we're sorted through him,

The way, the truth, the life.

Day 15

The perfect XY

He covers our chromosomes in a chrome of righteousness.

The perfect XY X-tends to me adoption papers
The perfect XY X-cludes none;
Y?
Cos the perfect XY lived, then didn't, but then did so this XY truly can.

The perfect XY chromosome rolled away the stone which changed everything;
Y?
Cos his resurrection breathes life into my soul.

XY in make-up
He makes up for our mistakes which makes us meet our Maker.

XXs and XYs no longer bound with an XX next to their name;
Y?
Cos the perfect XY X-tinguished the hold of sin
which is in our in-stinct.

At the X-act time
The perfect XY X-ercised perfect life
And X-changed breath for death;
X-changed my life for his
My outcome for his
My end point for his
My fate;
Y?
All to wipe away my disgrace before the Father's face.

Day 16
Work

Even God rested.

When it comes to work,
I wanna work at it.
I wanna come up with a working strategy so my work's effective.
So when I come to the end of a working day – the work I've worked on really does
… work!!!

The only thing I need to work at
is working off the clock,
after hours and taking my work home with me.

Cos soon as I put my key in the door (that won't work)
I remember all the work that's yet to be done and it works me up!
It's then that I work out my working strategy needs to be worked on.

Got to leave it at the workplace and come up with a relaxation strategy, one that
works for me.

One that lets me wind down and pick up work the next day.

And for my rest time?
I want my 'any other business' to be 'nobody else's business but God's business!!'

After all, whether 9-5, 24/7 or night shifts – take some tips from the Boss, the em-
ployer of all the employers – love work? Hate work? Rest and put God at the centre.
Otherwise you'll stop working … you'll be worked out.

Postmodern Psalms of Praise

As we read the psalms from the likes Of Asaph, Solomon and David, we learn that in their most basic form they can be stripped back to two categories: psalms that praise and psalms that pray. In our faith we in turn do both.

When life's great and God provides, we praise him and give him all the glory that's owing to him. Apostle Paul's a great example of how we should communicate to our living God – he (nearly) always starts his Epistles with what he is thankful for.

The truth is, the God we serve is sovereign, majestic, divine and perfect. In fact, if we collected all the perfect adjectives from all the languages the world has to offer, played them on a radio frequency that was set to loop – and let it resound forever, we'd probably be accused of few words. I like that. I like the fact that my God is so worthy to be praised for all he is – in his character, his divinity and all the 'Omnis' owing to his name. But what wows me is that this very being chose to humble himself and become human. The life of Jesus; the most beautiful, yet most significant act of compassion and sacrifice this world has seen and will ever see.

Sometimes, as life gets rough, we can lose sight of how great he really is. So, I guess the challenge is, whether life is full on fantastic or gut wrenchingly hard, whether our situation is hunky dory or not, to praise him regardless. And so we should remember – he is always worthy to be praised.

Day 17

You are

Mmmate,
Dad,
Lord,
God,
Alph,
Omeg,
You are
My heart,
My soul,
All that to me and more.

You are the sight of in-sight,
You're the winner of the spiritual warfare fight,
To you there is no darkness for you are the ultimate light.
You get me out of a pickle when things get a little tight.
Even though we disagree sometimes I know you're always right.

You are the almighty might,
The world-class author who breathed breath in men to write.
You are the immeasurable height.

Mmmate,
Dad,
Lord,
God,
Alph,
Omeg,
You really are …

Day 18

Your love rescues me

… And, boy, did I need rescuing.

Your love rescues me - completely.
Your grace gives me a second chance - full stop.
Your compassion is fully committed to me – genuine.
Your mercy humbles me – serious.

Your DNA is embedded in me – no joke
Cos you are my Creator – fact.

Your love for life tunes me up – proper time.
Your action of sacrifice blows me away – I mean it.
Your sovereignty excites me – big time.
Your example of a servant heart catches my attention – definite.

The reality of you wows me – most def,
The reality of you wows me – most def,

The reality of you wows me … end of.

Day 19
Director of the respiratory system

He is the director of the respiratory system,
He is the producer of the gravitational pull,
He's the head mechanic of metaphysics.

He's not just the mathematician who invented numbers,
He invented some guy called Pythagoras who put two and two together.

He is the artist who no one can brush up against
Or paint in a bad picture that is truly reflective.

He's the conductor of the symphony of existence,
And the composer of the constellations,

And he is so so much more than this limited intellect can fathom …

The poet of the deepest, most soul quenching verse and prose that has ever and will ever be written.

He's all that and then some.

Day 20

J to the C

Just a few ways to explain my awesome Saviour.

He's the king of kings
The lord of lords

The universal moulder
All life's secrets holder
And every moon, star and planet owner (gassy or rock)– in every solar system and every solar system in every galaxy.

If he wanted to, he could've made universe with a plural.
He is big, bigger than big, before time, after time, during time – all at the same time.

He's Unfathomable
Rationally Indescribable
Incomprehensible
And Logically Inconceivable.

He is the 'I AM'
The ultimate lamb
And he's the one who can
Do immeasurably more than all we can ask or possibly imagine.

He is higher than any height restriction.
He is the perfect athlete but he comes in last
The funniest comic – but gets heckled off the stage
He's the universal greatest but he gives it all up so I can really live.

He's fully filled with full on sovereign majesty
Yet he's still all about complete sacrificial humility.
Who is he?
He's J to the C.

Day 21

I stand

Wherever I am in life – there are countless reasons why you, God, should always be at the core of it.

I stand – in your truth.
I kneel - because of your love that breaks the bondage of sin.
I lay – pleading to be immersed in your peace that transcends all understanding.
I sit – at the foot of the cross.
I walk – knowing you're right beside me.
I run – for you, with you and towards you.
I sprint – I do it again … faster.

I skip – cos sometimes no words express you.
I jump – trying to reach you, but know I will never get high enough.
I hop – because you're the God of fun.
I free run – (badly) but do it cos I know you're the God of adventure.

I stand
I kneel
I lay
I sit

I walk
I run
I sprint
I skip

I jump
I hop
I free run
A bit

I sleep
I rest
I eat
I speak

I shout
I fight
I hide
I keep

I hit
A wall
I fall
I break
You mend
Me back
You make
Me fit.

Day 22

If we only knew

We couldn't box in how great God is if we tried.

If I could access a glimpse of your greatness
If I could get past your personal security
If I could go mission impossible and Tom Cruise my way through the heavenly air
vents … If I read the first word on the first page of the introductory book for begin-
ners on how magnificent you are … I'd crash with information overload.

We don't know the half of it.
We don't even know half of the half of it …
Or the half of that!

That you are great,
magnificent,
… (Enter word, which hasn't been invented to describe you)

If I could see things how the angels see things I'd fill my lungs with thanksgiving
harmonies and not even come up for air.

If I caught a glimpse of how you do relationship
My whole life cycle would be different.

If I could contain a milli-fraction of your divinity,
my life savings' worth of pennies would drop on how much you actually gave up.

We don't know the half of it.

Day 23
Something good

God is something good.

Something good is his goodness that is too good for anyone but accessible for everyone.

Something good is the smell of sweet sweet freedom which we don't deserve.

Something good is the piggy back rides I get when my feet can't take the pace.

Something good is the feel good sensation that arrives when I twig that no matter how many times I screw up, God's always ready to make up and win me back.

Something good is God's great grace that gratifies my soul.

Something good is scripture - the texture of text and the danger of depth that challenges me and changes me.

Something good is how he always lends an ear, how he always listens, and how he always, always does.

Something good is how he gets me more than I will ever get.

Something good is God.

God is something good -
whichever way you put it – still doesn't do him justice.

Day 24

He chooses me

He knows our flaws and failures. But he picks us and loves us regardless.

He chooses me
Handpicks me.

I try and convince him it's a wrong move -
I'm not who you think I am,
You've got the wrong guy.
There must've been a mix up with your heavenly filing system.

But he chooses me
Handpicks me
He selects me
He invests in me.

He chooses me
He knows me
And he gets me
And although he knows me
He doesn't drop me.

But he chooses me
Handpicks
Selects
And invests …

in me.

Day 25

He is my

He is our sustenance at all times.

He is my conveniently placed mattress when my knees give way.
He's my pat on the back when I can't do nothing right.
He's straight in with the Kleenex when I can't hold back the tears.

He's my five a day to get me through whatever I face.
He's my energy bar to get me over the finishing line.
He's my pep talk when I'm feeling rock bottom.

He's my turbo boost when I'm getting nowhere fast.
My bump start when my battery's flat.

He is my all
If I treat him that way or not.
He is - most certainly.

Day 26
The only shout out worth shouting about

He's most certainly worthy to be praised.

To the one who rescues me and makes me new
To the one who lets me off the hook
And doesn't let me stew.

To the one I hid from, but the truth he already knew.

Cos of his mercy, I make it;
I make it by meeting the mediator.

He saves me, frees me and gives me my identity.
His love is festering inside the depths of me
And it changes me.

Cos of his mercy, I make it;
I make it by meeting the mediator.

You were there –
You gave me life in despair.

Cos of his mercy, I make it;
I make it by meeting the mediator.

Postmodern Psalms of Prayer

When David's not busy composing praise through string arrangements, giving God his full on appreciation, he's wrestling with the nitty gritty of life and faith. To live a journey of faith with God is to involve him in every nook and cranny of our lives.

It's to communicate; stay in touch with him, to hear him speak to us through his God breathed scripture and talk back as we pray. To be thankful, yes – but to be real, raw and honest - not afraid to ask for whatever comes under his perfect plan.

Prayer is to be thankful and broken, to vent and reflect, to wrestle and pray for others. Prayer is what keeps us connected with the Father. When I feel distant from God, it's often because for one reason or another – I haven't made the effort to stay in touch.

But I think we should remember, there's nothing too big or too small to take to our God. Why? Because he's always up for a chinwag, not just for the sake of prayer time that resembles a shopping list, but to do relationship the way we were made to; full on intimacy with our maker.

He's the place we can go where we can be truly us. What's the point in hiding behind a spiritual mask when he knows our deepest thoughts and fears anyway?

When I think of prayer, I think of that great passage in Philippians 4:6-7 where Paul says …

'Do not be anxious about anything, but in every situation, by prayer and petition, with thanksgiving, present your requests to God. And the peace of God, which transcends all understanding, will guard your hearts and your minds in Christ Jesus.'

So, saying that - here are some of my psalms of prayer. Hope you enjoy.

Day 27

Fix me

We're all broken one way or another. We all need fixing.

Fix me, Lord; give my heart a makeover –
Cos right now it looks like a hangover.
New haircut,
New wardrobe,

I crave it, Lord,
but for the inside;
the heart,
soul
and spirit,

the bits that count.

Let my diet be Jesus.

Detox my soul
Tighten up my bolts
Stretch out my aches and pains
I want more of your pep talks.

Fix me
Fuel me
Restore my true identity
Navigate and enrich me,

So I can be all you destined me to be.
Forgiving Father -
Fix me.

Day 28

Elevate

Who are we living for ... us or him? (This poem works on different levels.)

I want me 'n' him to be in 2 elevators;
Him going up
And me
Going
Down.

It's never about me
But it's all about you.

Forgive me for wanting all the fame
when it should be about your name.

I want me 'n' him to be in 2 elevators;
Him going up
And me
Going
Down.

I want to re-address my priorities,
Do a spring clean on my lifestyle
'til what I'm left with are your priorities.

I want me 'n' him to be in 2 elevators;
Him going up
And me
Going
Down.

I want to never be in want.
I want to body pop the Spirit.
I want it to run through all my joints
So I can move how the Spirit wants me
to.

I want my only fix to be your Word,
And I want to be addicted to the stuff.
Cos I know I'm a mess without it.

Like I said,
2 elevators;
Him going up
And me
Going
Down.

Day 29

My prayer

Spiritual fitness, Christ-like discipline.

It's time to strive faster
To take bigger strides
To train more
To take the one and only holy protein shake
To listen to my trainer
To get my technique down
To warm up and warm down
To not get complacent
Or comfortable
Nor convenient,
To break past the pain barrier
To break a sweat
To not give up
Even if others are training harder
Or making more personal bests,
To knuckle down
To get the medal for my coach
To know what the medal is.
It's not just the metal round my neck.
It's the steps it took to get me onto the podium.

Day 30

Lord, give me ...

An honest prayer list.

Give me the heart to have compassion for others.

Give me the knowledge to make sense of your logic.

Give me the discernment to know when to use it.

Give me the vocab to know what I'm talking about.

Give me mercy to let others off the hook.

Give me strength to be weak and vulnerable.

Give me the humility to stop rubbing it in people's faces.

Give me the focus to stop making it about myself.

Give me perspective to not lose sight of things.

Remind me to forget what's not important.

Configure and reboot my hard drive when there's a system error.

Day 31

Lord, I feel like a double ...

You see through the act but still accept us.

Lord, I feel like a double,
A fake,
A cheaper version of the genuine article.

It's not all for show
But I just want you to know
The bits that other people see
Aren't even close to the really real complete me.

I feel like a con artist.
If only they knew
If only they knew me as you know me.

I guess that's what makes your love and acceptance that much more incredible.
It's cos you do
Know me for me
But you still don't stop loving me.

Cos underneath the whole façade of no problems Christianity,
With no doubt faith,
No temptation lifestyle,
No bad thought mindset,
Are real people.
And you love those versions of us too.
That is off the chart,
whichever scale you use.

Day 32

Your day/Your way

Dedicating the day to the one who is owed our everything.

Father,
Today is your day.
Your day to use me in whatever way
That you see fit.

I ask that you wipe the transgressions of
yesterday
The times where I went my way.
I pray that this day is clean slate day,

Another chance to give you my highest
thanks;
Not just with the words that I
pronounce
But through backing them up with my
actions.

Father, today
This day – it's your day.
Your day to use me your way.

I ask you to not see my sin
But to see your Son,
That I'm perfect and righteous in your
sight
Cos you judge me on his performance,
not mine.

Today, this day
I don't cross off the cross,
I highlight it and resonate on it.
Because of it
My Saviour's sacrifice saved me from
what should be my sentence.

Humble me to my knees before you
Wow me with fear and adoration of your
majesty
Bowl me over with your heart to know
me and to love me.

Today, Lord,
This is me giving my life
As a living sacrifice.

Cos this is your day
So I commit it to your way.

Day 33

Counting down the hours

Looking forward, but not losing sight.

I'm counting down the hours 'til I'm home.
'Til the realm of sin ceases to exist, but we exist in the realm of perfection.

Brokenness gets fixed
And pain gets ripped off like a plaster that's eternally disposed of.

A place where burdens are lifted, dismantled and returned.
A place filled to the brim with his glory, a place where eternity to praise him won't
seem like long enough.

Broken bodies get a Holy revamp
And blemishes are blotted out by the love of and for the Trinity.

I'm counting down the hours 'til I'm home dry,
Where I'm judged 'righteous' 'cos Jesus took my place as accused in the court before
the Father.

I'm eagerly awaiting paradise
Where tears only flow out of overwhelming awe and joy,
Where wars end
Where pain stops
Where burdens are lifted
And baggage is taken off our shoulders.

I'm counting down the hours 'til that day.
The day when I'm home,
Home dry.

But 'til that day,
I count every hour as time to give your name the praise.

Every hour, minute and second
A time to be salt and light.

I count every hour a time to start the fixing process that you'll ultimately finish.
Cos until I'm home,
I set up camp,
Cos there's work to be done
And every hour counts.

That being said, Lord - count me in.

Questions/Answers

If you have questions, does it make you less of a Christian? What about less holy? We all question from time to time, whether it's about pre-destination or something more controversial like 'how many rows of chairs to put out for the evening service'.

For some reason, somewhere along the line, most of us feel that we have to hide the fact that we question. I guess it makes us feel guilty or 'less holy'. As long as we look to the Bible for our answers and ask God to help our brains out in the understanding department, I think it's ok to have questions.

Without questions how can we grow in our faith? Without questions – we don't seek answers. When we don't seek answers, our 'walk' with God becomes more like a 'staying in one place while we tie our shoelaces' with God.

And I think he's up for us asking the questions. I guess it's just our job to make sure our hearts are in the right place to take the answers.

Here are some of my questions …

Day 34

What did you expect?

The Messiah the Jews expected probably didn't match up with Jesus' CV. What is it we expect?

What did you expect?
An overthrow of the Roman rulers?
A big show?
A staff,
A cape,
A colourful shaped 'J' with a sling and a stone?

What did you expect?
Identification?
A birth certificate with all the names under 'the son'?

What did you expect?
Everyone to get it?
100% proof
undisputable evidence
that this guy, Jesus, came straight from the heavens?

What did you expect?
Jews for celebrity fame,
Your mug shot to be on the front cover of Vogue?
In Jesus' name?

What did you expect?
For it all to make sense?

But how was it?
All of God's love, mercy and forgiveness compressed into skin and bone;
The guy who handcrafted existence, who hung up his rightful throne;

The rejected, strung out and executed who bled for my eternal freedom;
The guy who knows me by name and still loves me, though I screwed things up in the Garden of Eden.

Day 35

What's it all about?

If God sent us an e-mail update, maybe it would look a bit like this?

This world's not about you
It's about me.

It's about the penny dropping – who I
am.
Who am I?
The I am.

The love that outranks the damage of
any amount of sin.
I want you to love it
Cos the love I have cannot be measured.

They're all searching
But they're looking in all the wrong
places.
It's in their DNA to crave me
But they're fixing on all the wrong stuff.
I know they're searching cos I know
them …
by name,
personality
and
wrinkles – just like I know you.

And you?
You're my torches,
My fireflies in a pitch black forest.
So shine, be bright and flash your light
Cos right now they're in the dark.
But in me you can give 'em sight
And lead them to their heavenly Father
who's just wishing his kids would come
home.

You're my walking refrigerators in
a world where truth goes stale and
mouldy.
Preserve me
Don't throw away my message
But keep on to it.

Be my seasoning for the world.

Let 'em have a taster of me
By tasting you.

Day 36
Judge or be Judged?

We're judged by how much we judge others.

Which came first - Judge or be Judged?
Should I judge others for when I get a raw deal?
Should I raise my eyebrows when someone slips up and hurts me?
Should I?
Should I?
Should I?
Did he do it for me?
Let's see.

He lets you off the hook when you screw things up.
He gives you a second chance when his patience should be wearing thin.
He puts the 'wrong' records in the shredder when he could be attaching them on a mass e-mail.
He deletes the photos of what you did behind closed doors when he could've up-loaded them on Facebook.
He could've drawn out the forgiveness process and just let you sweat for a bit.
He could've played the 'you owe me big time' card.

You deserve it
But he didn't
But he doesn't.

He doesn't make you beg or squirm.
He doesn't lay the guilt trip on extra thick,
Heck, he doesn't even spread it on thinly.

Every time you royally mess things up
He doles out the vast quantities of second chance cards.

So, which came first?
Judge or be Judged?
To be Judged came first – but we don't get the sentence.

So, when you get the chance to put someone away
Remember, the head warden let you walk right out of the prison gates.

'To Judge' doesn't come first.
It doesn't even come second.
It just doesn't come.
Case closed.

Day 37

Which Luke do you want to be?

It doesn't get much worse than a Luke Warm faith.

I don't want to be Luke, Luke Warm.
I want to be Luke Fuh-fuh-fuhFreeeezing;
Preserving the Word of God,
Keeping it fresh so it doesn't go out of date.

And as well as being Luke, Luke Fuh-fuh-fuhFreeeezing,
I want to be Polar;
Not bear
but opposite!

I want to be Luke 'Flaming hot',
A Luke on fire for God
With a passion burning through the depths of my soul.

To be Fuh-fuh-fuhFreeeezing,
Never letting God's truth go stale and mouldy in me.
To be on fire,
A furnace of high temperatures.
He's my central heating
And I want his truth and love
To radiate through me
So I can warm other Lukes up
So they get fired up passion too!

Freezing, Fuh-fuh-fuhFreeeezing the fresh Word
But in the heat – melting my heart for what your heart melts for.
Cos I don't want to be just Luke – Luke Warm.

I want to be 'Fuh-fuh-fuhFreeeezing'
                    'Flaming hot'.

What about you – which Luke do you want to be?

Desert Place

Many biblical characters went through a desert place
(and we're not just talking literal here).

Moses spent 40 years trudging through a desert – 40 years of the physical meeting the metaphorical as the Jews are exiles from Egypt trying to figure out where their promised land is.

We got Joseph; his desert place was being left for dead by his older brothers and then sold on as a slave for a couple of quid.

And then there's David who spent half the psalms between a rock and a hard place.

The great thing is we can look back on all these characters and see God's unfolding master plan at work right from the offset.

David may have dropped a few balls when he committed half the crimes available in the space of a few days, but even so, God's love and mercy seeps out and he gets the promise of the Messiah running through his family tree.

Joseph? Well, even if he was his old man's favourite and his coat was all the rage in Paris at the time, he probably could've done with a bit more tact and a prescription of anti-ego tablets. Instead he showboats and rubs it in his brothers' faces.

Still in the rut, God shows up and next thing you know – Joey goes from slave in chains to Prime Minister in a suit.

And as for the Jews – they may have grumbled their way through the desert, but come a generation and a few tablets later, they reached the promised land.

However, as potentially insightful as all this is, we can't talk 'desert place' without mentioning a bloke called Job. With all the previous characters we can see that in some way, they had what was coming to them – after all, God is a just God. But then you look at Job – his heart was in the right place, he was a man of integrity – why did he deserve such pain and misery? He didn't. 'Course you know the story, don't you? Job ends by having a rant at God - why this and why not that? And then God comes back with – who are you to question what I do and do not do?

(Thought pause …)

We need to remember that even when we don't know, God knows what's going on. We need to trust in him, that he's got it all mapped out. But I don't think God is on any kind of vendetta for us making the fruit salad with the wrong fruit back in Genesis 3. Because all this time, his ultimate plan has been giving everything up, his son – even to death on a cross. Why? Because he loves us, and so we get relational restoration. Sometimes, we've got to trust that he knows what he's doing, even when we don't.

But having said all of this, I love how scripture gives us permission to question and to wrestle with God. Sometimes, we're not going to know the answers – but the one answer we should know and never forget is that God is with us … even when it feels like he isn't.

Day 38

Be raw, be real, be you

Just because we put our hope in the one who saves us, doesn't mean we're not saved if at times we question 'why?' through it.

Why the fronts?
The picture perfect faith where 'nothing bad happens cos you've got God on your side'.

If you're joyful,
scream it from the rooftops and mass e-mail your whole address book so everyone knows about it.

But if you're in the pits,
don't suppress it with guilt-filled grinning.
If you're down and almost out,
if it feels like no one's listening,
let him know,
let him have it …

Cos if you blame God and it's not his fault,
If it feels like he's just not returning your prayers,
If you can't see a way out –
Be raw,
Be real,
Be you.

He loves, he knows, he gets it.
And he's God – I think he's big enough to handle it.

Day 39
I'm flat

Life's not always plain sailing. But when we're feeling the pressure, there's always someone who's ready to listen.

My hazards are on
I've worn through the rubber
And now my timing belt has buckled under the pressure.

I'm worn out
My tread has left
My tyre's flat.
My alloys they've …
Been nicked, been swiped,
My flat's been knifed.

My spare's in use
My jack's no use
The lever's broke
I'm knackered
No good.

Broken down on the hard shoulder but people keep giving me the cold shoulder.

My hazards are on
I've worn through the rubber
And now my timing belt has buckled under the pressure.

My gasket's about to blow
My carburettor's seeping
My radiator's leaking
My oil level is dire.
And to top it all off
I've got a flat
I've got a flat tyre.

Desert Place : Poetry In Motion

My hazards are on
I've worn through the rubber
And now my timing belt has buckled under the pressure.

Oh Lord,
I'm worn out
Right through the rubber.
Forgive me for when I don't keep up the regular check-ups.
I feel like a dipstick that can't check the oil level
Cos I'm not reading the instruction manual
designed for me
and written by you.

But you're my recovery,
My greased up mechanic who offers his full service.
Thank you that you'll always take me in.
And thank you that you're always open for repairs, (especially on a Sunday).

Day 40

Let him in

He wants all of us, even the stuff we think he's not interested in.

Give everything over to him –
Big
Small
Mid
Long
Extra Extra
Thick or
Thin

Give it all over to him.

Let him in,
Let him on,
Let him in.

Let him in when you're too stubborn to ask for help;
Let him take over when nothing makes sense and you're just walking in the dark.
When you've got nowhere to turn - just look up.
When all you're feeling is space between you and him –
Let him on and let him in.

Talk to him – when nobody else is listening,
Give it to him – no matter what size, section or sorting code.
Give him all your anxiety, all your burdens and insecurity.
All your arrogance and ignorance
All your pride - let him sort it.
Give him your all – your pressures, your mess, your gift mix and your weak spots.

Give it all over – let him on and let him in.

Day 41
Out of place

No matter how much we feel out of place, he deliberately made us; as we are.

I feel miscellaneous
Like a spare wheel.

I feel like the extra screw from my IKEA bookshelf.
I feel understood in an
'I make no sense' kind of way.
I feel like a spare, spare wheel – one that doesn't even get to be spare!

A hammer that's got nail-o-phobia.
I feel out of place
Like sun stroke in a snow storm.

I feel over kill
Like a Tippex pen for a pencil when the rubber's already solved the problem.

Though he doesn't see me as spare.
He sees me as unique, wonderful and rare.
He sees me as extraordinary.

And he sees me
And smiles and tells me
I'm not forgotten
Nor misunderstood
Cos he made me;
I'm his
And I'm marked by his print.

Day 42

It figures

When nothing makes sense, when you just feel frustrated and you want to vent –
well, this is me doing just that. You could call it a Job moment.

I'm trying to figure something out.
Do the sums in my head and come up with the answer –
I just don't know what the sum is.
I mean nothing seems to fit or make sense.

I'm trying to get a grip but my palms are sweaty,
I'm trying to love but my heart is lonesome,
I'm trying to give but I've got holes in my pockets,
I'm trying to live but I need resuscitating.

I'm going fishing but I'm the worm on the hook,
I'm trying to escape but I'm turning myself in,

I'm living on the edge in a perfect circle,
I'm the tails on a double-headed coin.

I have a good balanced diet of eating junk food,
I live for laughs but don't have a sense of humour.

A dentist with false teeth
The chief exec who's on minimum wage
The chameleon who stands out like a sore thumb
The sore thumb who …?

JD without Turk
Dick Dastardly without Mutley
Gloves without fingers
Credit cards without interest

Paper without a pen
A pet without an owner
A fret board without a capo

A heart with nothing to pump
An ironic obsolete
A poem without a pun.
I'm trying to figure something out.
Do the sums in my head and come up with the answer –
Though maybe some sums are too complex to work out;

The equations too mind blowing to grasp.

Maybe we just have to trust
That he is the answer.

Topics

Some topics need their own ... 'topic' altogether.

Here are some topics which I have thought on and tried to communicate the best way I can. If you're in a church service, a small group or a dinner party – here are some poems on topics which might come in handy. If it's as an 'add on' to your sermon notes or just a poem to enter into a time of worship, I hope some of these help.

Day 43

Rich (Wealth)

When we lose perspective of what being rich really means.

I've got all things but I've got nothing.

I've got more than I could ever want yet I walk 'n' talk and live 'n' breathe like a hobo.
I dress well but I'm spiritually skint.
I look fancy but my mindset is homeless.

I'm full of wise words but I've had no life experience.
I'm on a journey but I never leave my own 4 walls of understanding.

I'm screwed on but I don't get it.
I can't fit my humble head through the doorframe.

I've got everything but I've got nothing.

I'm rich but when it comes to trusting God I'm over the overdraft limit.
I tithe 10% but the other 90 – hands off.

I'm rich but I'm in the red,
I'm full up but I'm still hungry.
I'm happy but I'm discontent.
I've got all things but I've got nothing.

Day 44

Justice (Justice)

We're called to want what God wants. And what he wants is his kingdom come
and will be done. Let's actively live it out.

I want to be hooked on Justice
Who's obsessed with selfless giving.
A man who never goes cold turkey on faith.

I don't want to be comfortable
I want to be gut wrenchingly on fire for God.

To get laid out to self
And to be made up in Jesus.

No longer comfortable
But immersed in his love and compassion
And never ending forgiveness.

To be led by the Spirit
To be uncomfortable.

Let us fight the Western virus
Of self-centred-ism;

No more self-satisfaction
No more self-serving
But more self-gratification in serving others.

I want to see Justice
In this place, that place
And that place next to this place.
In the place of my gripes where everything's all about me.

More restoration
More loving thy neighbour
whoever that is.

Less being about the problem
And more being a part of the solution.

No more degrees of separation
Where others' misfortunes are but a sigh in the 6 o'clock news' slot,
Or a £5 direct debit to fix our conscience clot.

More God
More of you
And less of us.
More of you in us,
With us.
And give us
Your strength to do your will to see your kingdom come.

Live in us,
The centre of us
As we surrender us
to your authority.

More your kingdom come
More of hope -
No, wait – more belief in the hope you have to offer
So more of your hope we filter to others.

The hope that transforms lives
And saves souls.

More of you
More of you
And less of us
Less of us – passing the buck on to you,

But more
More of us
Living for more of you.

Let people reside in you
Find their hope in you;
Let them confide in and set aside time to the King of all kings.
Cos you deal with our sin
And major in forgiving.

Day 45
It's not (Grace)

A syllable to pronounce, an eternity to be thankful for.

It's not something you can pick off the shelf.
Not from Marks and Sparks, Sainsbury's or Tesco's ...
No matter how many Extras it's got.

You can't purchase it on Amazon
Or do a swap on e-Bay.

You can't download it off i-tunes.
It can't be googled
And you can't add it as a friend on Facebook.
No matter how many hits, or wall posts –
It's 'www.notavailableonline.com'.

You don't find it on TV
Sky
Digital
Sky +
Sky digital Digital +.
If you've got a personal satellite to pick up channels right across the Milky Way –
don't bother looking, it's not there.

It's not earned like a pact between two Afghan soldiers
Or sold as clutter in a car boot sale.

You can't throw your paycheque @ it to get it
Or win it at a casino
Even if you have got a great hand.
It's got 'black jack' to do with luck.

You can't acquire it with fancy letters after your name
If you got a BA
        MA
        MBE
        I before E except after C;

   if you're MD,

MP,
PM
or just PMT –

There's no 'front of queue' treatment here i.e.
… put your name badges away.

It's not down a bottle
up a needle
in a magazine
or at a festival.

It's not on a 'going places' holiday package,
Even if it is in Hawaii
In a 5-star
All-inclusive
… So leave your mug passport photo in the drawer cos you won't get it on a plane.

It's not in mosques, masses or morning church services.

If you've got it all in life and then some –
If your home interior makes the Sistine Chapel look like a first draft -
It don't matter how hot
What you got
Or on popularity if you've hit the top

You've not got and you've got not … sqwat.

If you're on first term names with good ol' Bill down Microsoft
Or if you've pocketed the flashiest gadget,
It holds i-nawt in the bigger mega pixel.

If you get the whole mc^2 thing
And Newton's gravity fruit salad,
What's the point cos it can't be rationalized with any amount of IQs?

There's not a bribe, tip or bargaining chip
On the planet that can sort you out for it.

You can't earn it
                buy it
Win, borrow or lend it.

It's Unreachable
It's Unattainable

And it surpasses common sense.

I'm talking the real good news.
It's the G stuff,
Straight from the guy in the clouds.

And it's yours.
No ties, no legal tricks,
no small print.
Yours,
Free of charge … if you want it.

So what is it?

In the words of Frosties' very own Tony the Tiger …

It's … Grrrace.

Day 46
Map it out (Choice)

One choice holds our eternal outcome. The ball's in our court.

Life is but a fraction
A slice of
A drip from
A tap on
The door of
A house on an estate, in a hamlet, by a village, just off town, outside the city.

Life is but an acquaintance,
A nod,
A small talk in the grander scheme of conversation.

It's the click of a finger,
A press of a button,
The flick of a switch.
It's an instantaneous ever pass-you-by type of journey.

The pop of a champagne cork,
The lifespan of a cracker toy,
The movement of a microsecond.

Life is a journey,
A small journey
Where you choose which postcode to tap into the sat-nav.

So, before you set off,
Before you put your handbrake down and release the clutch from biting point …
Have you decided?
Have you mapped it out …?
Which route are you going to take?

Day 47
3 in 1 (Holy Trinity)

So there's three but one, eh?

1 is 3
3 is 1
3 is Father, Spirit,Son.

3 is God most high – plural;
Is relevant to all
Be it slums, street, urban or rural.

3 is 1
1 is 3
1 is God's divinity.
3 shapes, 3 roles
3 moulds, 1 throne.

1 of 3
Son is 1.
Son became humble
Gave up what he had.
Son is the physical incarnation of his heavenly Dad.

Son did fall
Son did die
Son did resurrect
And rose highest of highs.

1 is 3
3 is 1
3 is Father, Spirit, Son.

3 is 1
1 is 3
1 of 3
The Spirit be …

Wavy? Maybe
But in us, with us
the Spirit be;
A marked seal for our soul's eternal destiny … (Ephesians 1 verse 13!)

1 is 3
3 is 1
3 is Father, Spirit, Son.

1 is 3
3 of 1
Is Father of creation …
You know? Made all things, mun!

God is 1
God is He
God won us back from Genesis 3.

God is love
Almighty thee
In 3 forms
And he has won me over.
The 3 in 1, has won over me.

Festive poetry

Bar Easter, Christmas is the time of year where we crave for that extra creative bit in our carol services. A big reason is because we have the great opportunity to invite Gospel conversation into the madness of shopping lists, overstocked fridges, a backlog of Christmas cards and Santa hats.

In a nutshell, Christmas is the time the whole world proclaims Jesus as their Saviour – if they know it or not. And so when the world is stripping through the wrapping paper and tucking into turkey with cranberry sauce, our job is to let them know exactly who they are celebrating.

Here are a few ways that can help you do this ...

Day 48
The real Christmas story

Believe it or not, Christmas isn't all about the jolly fat guy.

Christmas trees, fairy lights and candles
All shining brightly in the night time
With snowmen pictures on the mantle.

Cliff Richard and Aled Jones,
The great escape and festive garden gnomes.

Mary Poppins and her spoon full of sugar
That makes the medicine go down,
The unwrapped Nintendo wii that turns a smile from a frown.

Stuffed full with roasted parsnips and Queen's speech at three,
Turkey and stuffing sandwiches with Twiglets for your tea.

Christmas specials on the BBC, hence the family doth congregate
And the kids are doing your nut in after an over hyperactive state … 15 hours straight!

And so by now it's getting late.
The clock ticks past twenty-five past nine,
And Granddad's unconscious on the sofa after several glasses of mulled wine.

And so, before you know it,
The evening's nearly over.
You call Granddad a taxi cab
And Mum gets out the Hoover.

So, the kids are fast asleep
And the 6 am alarm clocks are set.
While Mum and Dad are outers,
dreaming over the Christmas monster -
Credit card debt!

So that's Christmas, in a nutshell, in a way.
I'm trying to think if there's anything left,
Anything I missed out,
Anything I didn't say.

No? So then –
Oh no - Wait!
I remember!
How could I forget?

I nearly missed the most crucial vital bit
And without it – Christmas wouldn't even be here to celebrate!

Known to millions around the world,
The story of one – more important than anything I mentioned before.
More so than snow, reindeers, elves
Or festive giving for the cause,
One guy made Christmas significant:

The one and only Santa Claus …
(That's not right – is it?)

Day 49

The *ickle* King of the Crib

Just a taster of how our Almighty became so vulnerable at Christmas.

Let me tell you of the ickle King of the Crib.

He commands more authority than every president who's ever lived … combined … times a billion.

He has more love to offer than a Led Zeppelin hit record.

The ickle King of the Crib
Was before,
Before the offset set off
Before matter even mattered.

He was the Chief Executive of Existence,
He was the Architect who designed the plans for the Grand Canyon
And the Structural Engineer who made it happen within a week.
He even gave the planning permission.

The King of the Crib
Became ickle, small and so vulnerable
He didn't have enough strength in his neck muscles to hold his head up.
He became freckles, moles, beauty spots and earlobes.
The King of the Crib became human; fully.
But still King over creation; fully.

The King of the Crib
Lived and breathed so we can breathe in new life,
A fresh start,
A clean Etch-a-sketch.

He was before
Is during
And will be ever after.

Cos the ickle King in the crib
By the donkey
And the prezzies,
With the shepherds
And their tea towels,
Was just the beginning.
Scene 1 on earth.

The ickle King of the Crib grew up.
He was complete compassion,
Not just born into birth
But dedicated to death … and beyond.
His sufficient sacrifice sorted my sin
As the Saviour sought after my heart.

So the ickle King of the Crib
Became King over death
King over my sin
King of my life
King Eternal.

Jesus, King of the Crib
Jesus, the King of my heart.

Day 50
X marks the spot

Let's not take Christ out of Christmas.

X marks the spot.
It marks the spot of X-tra curricular festive activities,
Sky + put to good use and cases full of DVD box-X.

X-factor marks the spot
With BIG drama, the voice over man
And Louis' class acts that go very nice with crackers and wine …
(You know … cheese),
While X-tra, X-tra, everyone's 'reading all about it' -
Who's going to mark the X-mas no 1 spot?

X-box 360 … live marks the spot –
With X-ilerating game play – only £239 this X-mas!

X marks the spot-mas.
X-mas tree with fairy lights and games 'n' prezzies on the floor;
With mulled wine, monster truck toys, marketing ploys, and mistletoe.

X marks X-cruciatingly bad Christmas cracker jokes,
And paper hats and a false moustache, with the small screwdrivers which you swear
will come in handy every year but are in the bin before you can say,
'The Only Fools and Horses X-mas special is on the telly!'

X marks the carol singing spot
With 'We wish you a merry X-mas and a happy new year'.
And so, come 25th of December
X-mas marks the spot-mas.

And even though a name (that shall remain nameless) was swapped for X,
This 'X' was marked on a cross
And this 'X' took my spot.
But let's not say it.
Let's just say 'X'.
After all, X wouldn't want to make anyone feel X-tremely ve-X'd,
nor even slightly uncomfortable.
X would rather just stay quiet in the background this X-mas.
And it's ok - X understands …
Saying … Christ at X-mas.
It's a bit politically incorr-X.

Dai Woolridge works for Christian charity 'Going Public' which is based in Cardiff. It is committed to investing in every one life it comes across, so they believe in their intrinsic worth.

A creative resource for the church through theatre, storytelling, comedy, poetry and performance;
all to communicate His saving grace to a lost and broken world.

'Getting gritty and witty with professional theatre stuck in scripture ...'
Grit – to create and perform with passion.
Wit – to engage through humour and comedy.
Professional – to produce quality and original material for the masses, that won't look out of place in big fancy theatres.
Scripture – to be directly inspired by scripture personally and professionally. To not lose sight of the message and to remain faithful to it.

Website: www.goingpublic.org.uk/theatre
e-mail: gptc@goingpublic.org.uk
Twitter : @twitwitandgrit

Going Public Personal Social Education Department (PSE) ... Schools Work

'Education for personal wellbeing through the creative arts'

We visit secondary schools and youth groups across Wales and occasionally England covering topics that the PSE curriculum in schools has to cover.

We deliver a 45-minute theatre piece followed by either a 20-minutre or 40-minute workshop, along with a series of 'esteem lessons', plus five lessons as part of the 'Marvellous Me' package for sex education in primary schools.

'We are passionate about each one life we encounter and reminding young people of their intrinsic worth.'

'In Search of a Happy Ending'
Theme: Sex and Relationships
Aimed at: Year 9
Synopsis: The play follows the relationship between two 16-year-olds, Jack and Charley, as the couple search for their happy ending.
About: 'In Search of a Happy Ending' has a primary objective to educate and challenge pupils' sexual health and relationship choices, with a strong emphasis on healthy relationships.

'Wholehearted'
Theme: Self Esteem
Aimed at: Year 8 girls
Synopsis: The play follows the relationship of three (very different) teenage girls, Macey, Sally and Annie, who are a group of friends each learning how to cope with issues of self esteem, body image and friendship.
About: Wholehearted's primary objectives are to develop positive attitudes toward self and others, distinguishing the features of healthy friendships and relationships.

'Borderline Alcoholic'
Theme: Alcohol Abuse
Aimed at: Year 10
Synopsis: Borderline Alcoholic follows 20-year-old Dylan as we unpack his relationship with alcohol.
About: Following Going Public's usual style of a theatre piece followed by a workshop, it will educate young people on the effects of misusing alcohol and how they can make informed choices concerning their alcohol consumption.

'Snakes and Ladders'
Theme: Mental Health
Aimed at: Year 10 +
Synopsis: Snakes and Ladders follows a day in the life of Will, whose 'seeming' best friend is depression. Ultimately the piece journeys toward the hope that is always there.
About: Snakes and Ladders seeks to demystify the myths behind mental health issues such as depression, anorexia and self-harm. It depicts the endeavour to quiet the voice of the depressive's worst critic (depression) through a variety of therapeutic tools.

www.goingpublic.org.uk/schools

Going Public Training exists to train, mentor, disciple, equip and release people into their God-given potential as outward-looking disciples and leaders who will go on to invest in others.

We are committed to a **Head – Hands – Heart** philosophy and holistic learning.

Head: Quality information taken in via a collaborative learning environment.

Hands: A mentoring community to aid reflection on everything learnt and experienced.

Heart: Opportunities for many varied missional experiences.